WITHDRAWN

SPACE!

NEPTUNE

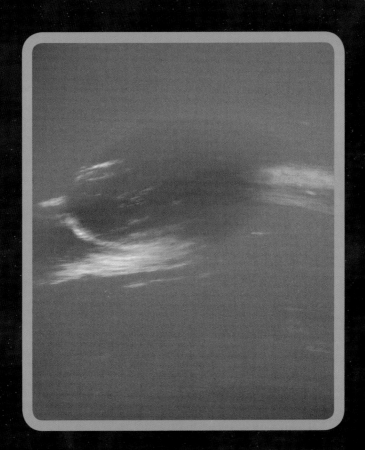

JOSEPHA SHERMAN

Marshall Cavendish
Benchmark
New York

Marshall Cavendish Benchmark
99 White Plains Road
Tarrytown, New York 10591
www.marshallcavendish.us

Library of Congress Cataloging-in-Publication Data

Sherman, Josepha.
   Neptune / by Josepha Sherman.
      p. cm. -- (Space!)
   Summary: "Describes Neptune, including its history, its composition, and its role in the
solar system"--Provided by publisher.
   Includes bibliographical references and index.
   ISBN 978-0-7614-4246-2
   1. Neptune (Planet)--Juvenile literature. I. Title.
   QB691.S54 2010
   523.48--dc22
   2008037279

Editor: Karen Ang
Publisher: Michelle Bisson
Art Director: Anahid Hamparian
Series Design by Daniel Roode
Production by nSight, Inc.

Front cover: A computer illustration of Neptune
Title page: Neptune's Great Dark Spot
Photo research by Candlepants Inc.
Front cover: Chris Bjornberg / Photo Researchers Inc.
The photographs in this book are used by permission and through the courtesy of:
NASA: JPL, 1, 4, 5, 16, 17, 22, 25, 28, 31, 37, 39, 44, 46, 47, 54, 56; JPL/USGS, 29; ESA, Y. Nazé
(University of Liège, Belgium) & Y.H. Chu (University of Illinois, Urbana), 43; VLT/ESO/
JPL/Paris Observatory, 51; 52; JPL/STScI, 53. Photo Researchers Inc.: Sheila Terry, 6, 7;
Royal Astronomical Society, 11; Detlev van Ravenswaay, 20; Seth Shostak, 21; Mark Garlick,
26, 27, 49; Chris Butler, 30; Lynette Cook, 31; David Nunuk, 38; John R. Foster, 55. The Image
Works: World History / Topham, 8, 9; SSPL, 12; Art Media / HIP, 15. Getty Images: Time
& Life Pictures, 24, 33, 18, 34, 40, 41; 36; Frank Whitney, 42. Illustration on page 48 by
Mapping Specialists © Marshall Cavendish Corporation.
Printed in Malaysia
123456

CONTENTS

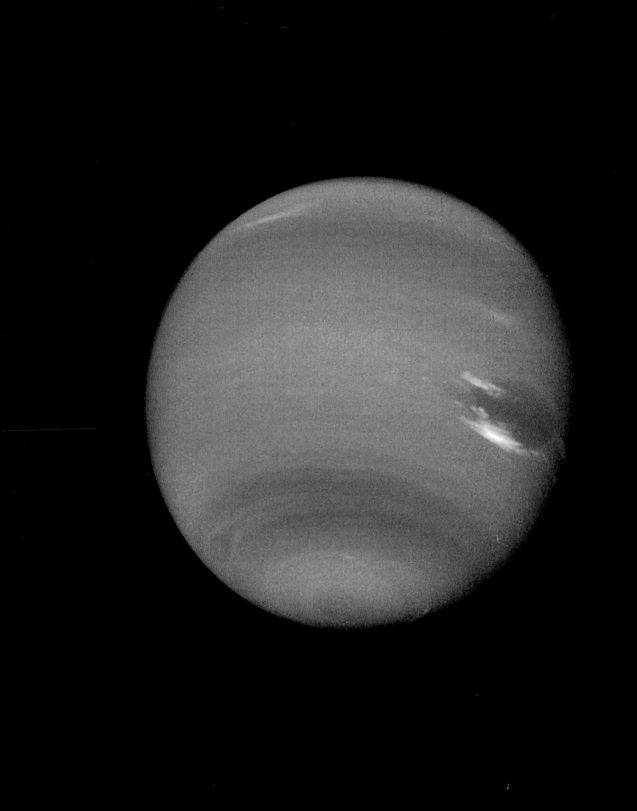

1

THE DOUBLE DISCOVERY

Toward the end of the eighteenth century, everyone believed that the Solar System contained only six planets. Then Uranus was discovered in 1781 by William Herschel. With this seventh-planet discovery, **astronomers** became more curious. What else might be out there?

THE SHEPHERD ASTRONOMER

The first scientist to predict the existence of an eighth planet was French astronomer Alexis Bouvard. Bouvard had an unusual background for a scientist. He was born in 1767 in the French countryside, did not attend school, and had been raised to be a shepherd. However, he was so interested in science that he ran

Even during its discovery in the 1800s, Neptune appeared as a bright starlike dot in the sky. Scientists got a better look at this eighth planet in the 1980s, when spacecraft flew by the planet.

away to Paris when he was a teenager. While in Paris—doing whatever odd jobs he could find—he taught himself mathematics. Bouvard was so intelligent that he soon became an assistant to another astronomer, Pierre Laplace.

By the 1820s, Bouvard was working as an astronomer and mathematician. He noticed that Uranus's **orbit** around the Sun showed some strange movements. Bouvard thought that the "wobble" must be caused by the **gravity** of another object pulling at Uranus. However, Bouvard would not be the one to discover that an eighth planet was causing the movements in Uranus's orbit.

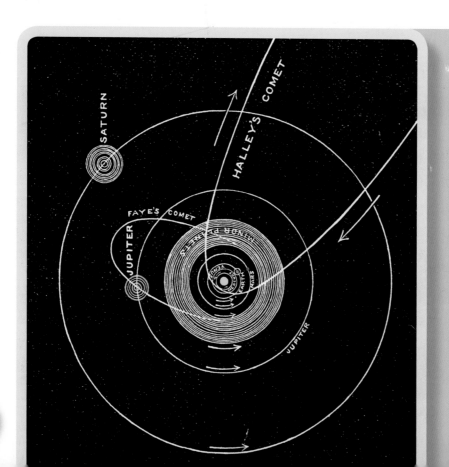

Early astronomers kept track of celestial objects by using star and planet charts.

Some astronomers during Bouvard's time used very large telescopes that had to be maneuvered using long ropes, wheels, pulleys, and other tools. But even those big telescopes could not produce images as clear as the ones we see today.

JOHN COUCH ADAMS

John Couch Adams was born in 1819 in Cornwall, England. Adams was very good at mathematics and quickly became fascinated with astronomy. In 1841, Adams first read about Bouvard's calculations of Uranus's orbit. The calculations made a great impression on him, and he was determined to discover what was affecting Uranus's orbit. On July 3, 1841, he wrote a note that said, "Formed a design . . . of investigating, as soon as possible . . . the irregularities in the motion of Uranus . . . to find whether they may be attributed to the action of an undiscovered

John Couch Adams came from a family of farmers, but once his parents realized how good he was at mathematics and science, they sent him to school to learn as much as he could.

planet beyond it." From then on, Adams spent all his free time working on the calculations that would prove his theory. By September 1845, he had his mathematical proof of a new planet.

Unfortunately, Adams was too shy to make a public announcement of his findings. Instead, he sent his papers to the head astronomer of England, Sir George Biddell Airy. But Airy completely ignored Adams' findings. Why he did so is a mystery to many historians. It is possible that Airy was overwhelmed by his own work, or perhaps he just failed to see the importance of Adams' calculations. Because Airy ignored Adams' findings, no one else in England at that time made any real effort to find out if there really was an eighth planet.

URBAIN J. J. LE VERRIER

Urbain Jean Joseph Le Verrier was born in the French province of Normandy in 1811. Le Verrier was a serious and intelligent student, fascinated by all branches of science. By 1837, he was working as an astronomer. Because he had a gift for mathematics, he threw himself eagerly into solving even the most complicated equations.

Le Verrier found errors in many of the planetary calculations and created more efficient methods for calculating orbits. On September 10, 1839, he submitted a paper to the Academie des Sciences (Academy of the Sciences) titled, *"Sur les variation seculaires des orbites planetaires."* (*"On the normal variations*

In addition to making important astronomical discoveries, Le Verrier worked as a director of the Observatory of Paris, where he oversaw the observatory's rebuilding and reorganization, making it a well-respected astronomical institution.

of planetary orbits"). Le Verrier continued to work on perfecting his calculations, but he also became fascinated with the movement of comets and began making studies of them and their orbits. By age thirty-four, in 1845, Le Verrier had already made a name for himself as a brilliant analyst of astronomical problems.

As soon as he noticed the odd movement of Uranus's orbit, Le Verrier set to work trying to find an eighth planet. He had never seen John Adams's work and did not know that Adams had also been looking for an eighth planet. Le Verrier had no way of knowing that his calculations were almost identical to those of Adams. But unlike Adams, Le Verrier was not shy. Le Verrier made sure that everyone knew about his calculations. On June 1, 1846, he presented his completed analysis, "*Recherches sur les mouvements d'Uranus,*" or "*Research on the movements of Uranus,*" at a public meeting of the Academy of Sciences.

THE BATTLE OVER THE EIGHTH PLANET

Back in England, Airy heard about Le Verrier's calculations and public announcement. Airy then realized how similar Le Verrier's findings were to the work of John Adams. England and France had been bitter political rivals for hundreds of years.

Naturally, Airy did not want France to gain the glory of finding that eighth planet. He organized a secret attempt to find the planet. In July 1846, he held a meeting with astronomer James Challis, who was the head of the Cambridge Observatory. Airy asked Challis to look for the planet with the observatory's telescope "in the hope of rescuing the matter from a state which is . . . almost desperate."

A frantic search ensued. Adams continued with his calculations but his new calculations were incorrect. Because Challis did not have an up-to-date star chart, he was often searching the wrong part of the sky. Historians now know that Challis did see Neptune twice—on August 8 and 12—but because of the problems with the old star chart and Adams's faulty calculations, Challis thought he was just seeing another star.

Meanwhile, in France, Le Verrier was having a problem, too. After he had publicly announced

In addition to being the first to view Neptune and identify it as a planet, Galle also discovered one of the inner rings of Saturn in 1838.

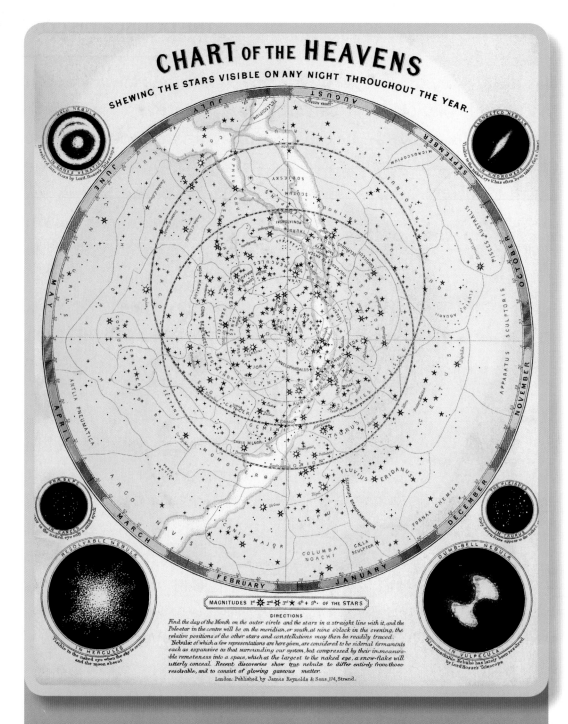

CHART OF THE HEAVENS

SHEWING THE STARS VISIBLE ON ANY NIGHT THROUGHOUT THE YEAR.

MAGNITUDES 1st ✸ 2nd ✷ 3rd ✳ 4th + 5th • OF THE STARS

DIRECTIONS

Find the day of the Month on the outer circle and the stars in a straight line with it, and the Polestar in the centre will be on the meridian, or south, at nine o'clock in the evening, the relative positions of the other stars and constellations may then be readily traced.

Nebulæ of which a few representations are here given, are considered as sidereal firmaments each as expansive as that surrounding our system, but compressed by their immeasurable remoteness into a space, which at the largest to the naked eye, a snow-flake will utterly conceal. Recent discoveries show true nebulæ to differ entirely from those resolvable, and to consist of glowing gaseous matter.

London: Published by James Reynolds & Sons, 174, Strand.

Early astronomers depended on star charts to help them identify celestial bodies. However, if a chart was incorrect, as was the case with the chart used by Challis, any astronomical findings made using the chart could be completely wrong.

his findings, he was disappointed to find that no French astronomer seemed to be interested in proving them. He then sent his calculations to a fellow scientist with whom he had been exchanging science papers. That scientist was the German astronomer Johann Gottfried Galle, who worked at the Berlin Observatory. Galle received Le Verrier's letter and paper on September 23, 1846. That same day, the excited Galle got to work. Using Le Verrier's calculations and working with the observatory's telescope and star atlas, Galle found the eighth planet after looking for only an hour. On September 25, Galle wrote to Le Verrier that, "The planet whose position you have pointed out *actually exists*."

A WAR OF WORDS

Galle's discovery launched a war of words between English and French scientists. The members of the English Royal Astronomical Society backed Adams, saying that he had been the first to calculate where the planet would be. Meanwhile, in France, the scientists there were furious. An unknown Englishman, they said, was trying to take away the credit that Le Verrier deserved. The French newspapers picked up the story and turned it into a national issue.

Adams finally decided that enough quarrelling had taken place. In a paper that he read before the Royal Astronomical

LATER HONORS TO ADAMS

Although his discovery of Neptune was at first ignored, Adams did not go unnoticed by the scientific community. In 1866, his work was honored when he won the highest award in English astronomy—the Gold Medal of the Royal Astronomical Society.

Today, Neptune's outer ring and a lunar crater on our Moon are named for Adams. There is also an asteroid named 1996 Adams. The Adams Prize is presented each year by the University of Cambridge, honoring Adam's work.

Society in November 1846, he said, "I mention these dates merely to show that my results were arrived at independently, and previously to the publication of those of [Monsieur] Le Verrier, and not with the intention of interfering with his just claims to the honors of the discovery." Adams added that there was no doubt that Le Verrier had published his research first and that those published findings had led to the actual discovery of the new planet by Galle.

Once the facts came out, astronomers began to agree that the two astronomers had each independently helped to locate a new planet and that they should share the fame. At first, French astronomers wanted to name the new planet "Le Verrier," but the calmer members of the scientific community voted that

In Roman mythology the god of the sea was called Neptune, but in Greek mythology, he was known as Poseidon.

name down. Enough time had been wasted quarrelling with their English counterparts. Everyone settled, instead, on the name Neptune, after the Roman god of the sea.

2

VOYAGER 2

On October 10, 1846—within a month after Neptune's discovery—British astronomer William Lassell discovered Triton, one of Neptune's moons. But after this, no new Neptune discoveries were made until the twentieth century.

There were two very good reasons for this. One was that telescopes built before the twentieth century simply were not strong enough to see Neptune as more than a bright spot in the sky—much like a star. The second reason was the fact that Neptune is so far from Earth. Scientists today calculate that it is about 2.82 billion miles (4.3 billion kilometers) away. It is so far away that it is the only planet that cannot be seen from Earth without a telescope. It was not until 1949 that anything new was learned about Neptune. That was when astronomer

Voyager 2's special imaging tools provided this colored image of Neptune, which shows a red haze around the planet. This haze proves that Neptune has a thick and gaseous atmosphere.

GERARD PETER KUIPER

This astronomer was born in 1905 in the Netherlands. Kuiper became an American citizen in 1937, when he also took a position at the Yerkes Observatory at the University of Chicago. Kuiper later moved to Arizona and founded the Lunar and Planetary Laboratory at the University of Arizona.

Kuiper made several important astronomical discoveries during his time in Chicago and Arizona. He discovered one of Uranus's moons, Miranda, and Neptune's moon, Nereid. He also found carbon dioxide in Mars's atmosphere and proved that there was a methane atmosphere surrounding Saturn's largest moon, Titan. To honor Kuiper's many discoveries, an award called the Kuiper Prize is given to astronomers who have made great advances in planetary sciences.

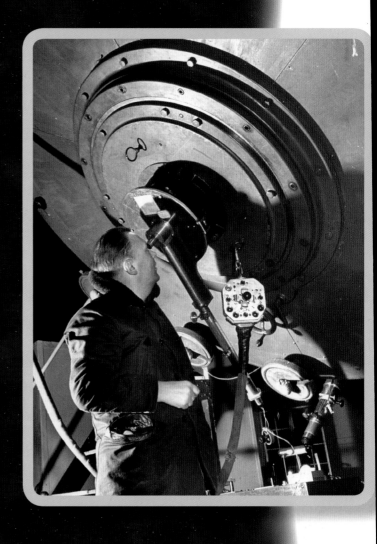

Gerard Peter Kuiper discovered another moon orbiting Neptune. He named it Nereid, after the Greek name for a sea nymph.

THE SPACE RACE

Later discoveries about Neptune and other objects in space were due to newer technologies and daring missions into space. Most developments in space technology and exploration are the result of a war with no real fighting. This was called the Cold War, and it was a rivalry between the United States and the Soviet Union. (The Soviet Union was made up of Russia and its conquered countries.) The Cold War lasted from 1945 to 1989. The United States and the Soviet Union "fought" the Cold War in many ways, including spying, military buildups, a dangerous nuclear weapons race, and the space race.

The space race began as a competition to be the first nation to put a **satellite** into orbit and then to put a man on the Moon. The Soviet Union was the first to successfully launch a satellite (*Sputnik*), in 1957. The United States countered by becoming the first to put men on the Moon in 1969.

Out of all the competition came a United States organization known as the National Aeronautics and Space Administration (NASA). NASA soon became primarily a science organization interested in **aviation**, space vehicles, life in space, and space exploration.

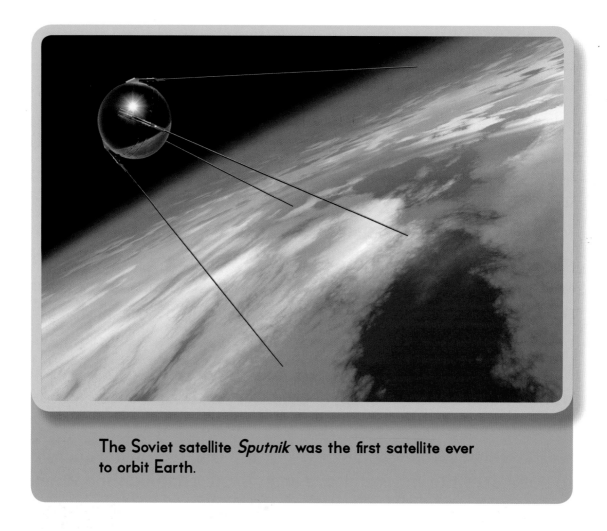

The Soviet satellite *Sputnik* was the first satellite ever to orbit Earth.

NASA remains active now even though there is no longer a space race. However, NASA is not alone. Other space programs exist throughout the world. The European Space Agency (ESA) is made up of scientists from several European countries. Other international space programs include the Italian Space Agency, the Japanese Aerospace Exploration Agency, and the Brazilian Space Agency.

VOYAGER 2

Neptune revealed more of its secrets with the help of the *Voyager 2* spacecraft. NASA and the Jet Propulsion Laboratory (JPL) worked together to design and build the *Voyager* program. Two identical unmanned—which meant no astronauts were inside—spacecraft, *Voyager 1* and *Voyager 2,* were launched in 1977 to explore Jupiter and Saturn. After the spacecraft were in space, their mission was changed to include observations of Uranus and Neptune before the spacecraft left our Solar System to explore the space beyond. *Voyager 2* was the first spacecraft to visit Neptune.

Voyager 2 traveled at about 42,000 miles (67,000 km) per hour faster than any manned spacecraft could go. However, the distance to Neptune is so great that it still took the

This illustration shows *Voyager 2* as it flies by Neptune. The Sun can be seen as a bright star in the distance.

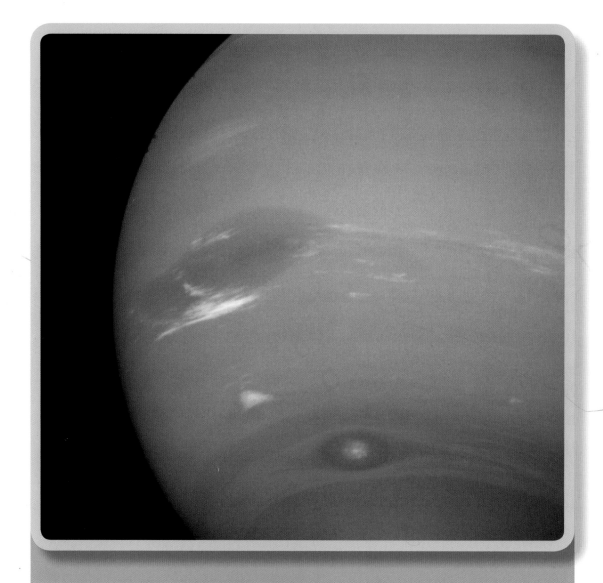

Voyager 2 provided scientists with clear images of the Great Dark Spot, Scooter, and the Dark Spot 2.

spacecraft twelve years to reach the planet. In 1989, *Voyager 2* got close enough to Neptune to start making observations. The spacecraft continued making observations from June through October. The closest it came to Neptune was on August 25, 1989.

Voyager 2 sent back some spectacularly clear data and pictures to scientists on Earth. The images and information showed that Neptune was somewhat similar to Uranus and Jupiter. Like them, it is a **gas giant** planet. Neptune also had methane in its **atmosphere,** giving the planet a blue color.

Voyager 2 also gave scientists their first look at a giant storm on Neptune, which they called the **Great Dark Spot**. That storm was as large as Earth. The Great Dark Spot moved around the planet every sixteen days as Neptune's powerful winds pushed it along. Recent observations of Neptune revealed that the Great Dark Spot has disappeared.

There was also a smaller storm system, which they named Dark Spot 2. It seemed to be caught in faster winds, because it traveled around the planet in only sixteen hours. With the Dark Spot 2 was a bright—almost white—cloud that scientists called Scooter because it "scooted" around Neptune in sixteen hours.

Voyager 2 provided scientists with so much information about Neptune. It confirmed that, like all the other planets, it had a **magnetic field**. Neptune's field is stronger than that

BOLDLY GOING INTO SPACE

The twin spacecraft, *Voyager 1* and *Voyager 2*, were launched by NASA in the summer of 1977 from Cape Canaveral, Florida. *Voyager 1* now holds the record as the spacecraft that has traveled farther than any other. *Voyager 2*, which visited more planets, including Neptune, is heading out there, too.

In another ten to twenty years, the *Voyagers* will continue on to cross the heliopause, which is the space outside our Sun's influence. They will keep going, with enough power to keep broadcasting back to Earth until at least 2020. *Voyager 1* and *Voyager 2* are destined to wander through our Milky Way galaxy eternally—unless they crash into something unknown. Each spacecraft carries a recording offering samples of Earth music and language and sending greetings to anyone who might find them.

The *Voyager 2* space probe.

A close-up image from *Voyager 2* shows the swirling, stormy clouds that make up the Dark Spot 2.

of Earth. Data from the spacecraft helped scientists calculate the accurate length of the Neptunian day. (A day is the time it takes for a planet to make a complete rotation on its **axis**.) From Earth, astronomers could only estimate it as being eighteen hours long. But *Voyager 2* proved that the Neptunian day lasts about sixteen hours and seven minutes.

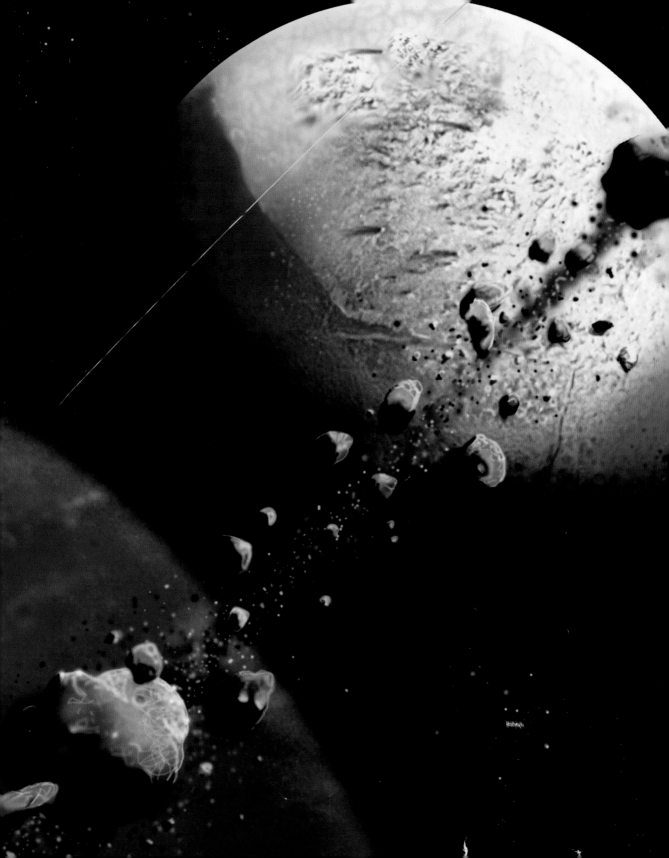

3

NEPTUNE'S STRANGE MOONS AND RINGS

Some of Neptune's features, such as its moons and rings, are strange and mysterious. Neptune has some very odd moons, ranging from the huge to the tiny. There is also the mysterious case of Neptune's disappearing rings. While *Voyager 2* gave scientists some clues about Neptune, there have been constant changes and discoveries since 1989.

NEPTUNE'S MOONS

Triton

Triton is so big that it could almost qualify as a planet itself. With a diameter of 1,681 miles (2,706 km), it is the planet's largest

An illustration shows Neptune (blue) with its largest moon, Triton, orbiting next to it.

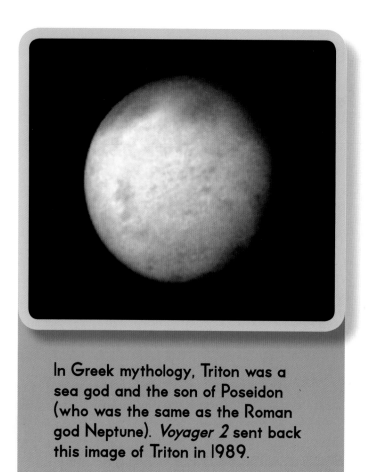

In Greek mythology, Triton was a sea god and the son of Poseidon (who was the same as the Roman god Neptune). *Voyager 2* sent back this image of Triton in 1989.

moon. Triton makes its complete orbit around Neptune in just under six Earth days. Triton has a **retrograde** orbit, which means it moves around Neptune in a direction opposite from the direction of the planet's orbit. Most of the other moons, including ours, rotate around their planets in the same direction as the planets.

Scientists have been trying to figure out why Triton goes backward. They think that this backward rotation means that Triton was not formed with Neptune, but was a separate moon or planetoid, which is a little planet. The moon or planetoid was probably pulled into Neptune's orbit once it came too close.

Scientists think that before Triton was captured by Neptune's gravity, it was moving fairly quickly through space—faster than a moon in orbit moves. So where did the extra energy go? In 2006, two astronomers—Craig Agnor of the University of California and Douglas Hamilton of the University of Maryland—came up with a theory that might be right. They think that Titan must have been wandering through space with another moon, locked in each other's gravity. When the two moons passed Neptune, the planet's greater gravity caught Triton but hurled the other moon away. Most of the extra energy would have gone off with that lost moon, and Triton would have settled into its reverse orbit around Neptune.

This illustration of Neptune from Triton's uneven surface was created based on *Voyager 2* images.

Weather on Triton

Triton may be the coldest object in our Solar System. Its surface is usually about -391 degrees Fahrenheit (-235 degrees C). However, when *Voyager 2* flew past it, the spacecraft discovered that despite the extreme cold, Triton has **geysers**—possibly of nitrogen and methane—that soar about 5 miles (8 km) up into Triton's thin atmosphere. On Earth, geysers are fountains of hot water. But anything hot on so cold a moon seemed impossible. Scientists think that the geysers might be caused by the planet's dark surface material absorbing heat from the Sun. Triton's surface cracks as its orbit takes it closer and further away from the Sun. Those cracks would allow the nitrogen under the surface to escape. It is also possible that the heat from the Sun is being stored through those cracks, just under Triton's surface. This would keep the nitrogen gas warm enough to sometimes erupt. Even the slightest heat would be enough to do that, since the rest of the moon is so cold.

Triton's geysers are made of heated nitrogen and methane.

Odd Looks

Triton is heavier and rockier than the other moons of Neptune and is covered with a coating of frozen methane. It is this methane ice that reflects light and makes Triton look very bright through a telescope. Unlike the other Neptunian moons, Triton also has its own faint atmosphere, which is a mix of nitrogen and methane. Triton has a polar ice cap like many planets, though in this case the ice is made of pinkish nitrogen.

Part of Triton's surface is so odd-looking and puckered that scientists call it cantaloupe terrain, because it looks like the surface of a cantaloupe. This kind of terrain has not been found

To many, Triton's dimpled and grooved surface resembles the skin of a cantaloupe.

on any other moon or planet. There are also stretches of smooth areas that might be the result of lava flows in the distant past. Triton has only a few impact craters, showing that it had not been hit by many meteors or other moons in its lifetime.

Since Triton does not look like any other moon, scientists think that it may actually have come from the **Kuiper Belt**, which is a collection of larger icy objects beyond Neptune. Objects in the Kuiper Belt orbit the Sun the way a planet does. Scientists think that the objects in the Kuiper Belt are ancient leftovers from the time when the Solar System first formed.

Astronomer believe that millions of i rocky objec fill the Kuip Belt. Some these objec have been identified as dwarf plane

Neptune's Other Moons

The *Voyager 2* mission revealed that Neptune had seven other moons besides Triton. With a diameter of approximately 250 miles (400 km), Proteus is Neptune's second-largest moon. It is one of the darkest celestial bodies in the Solar System and reflects very little sunlight. *Voyager 2* images showed that Proteus has an irregular and almost lumpy shape. Proteus is about 57,500 miles (92,800 km) away from Neptune's top cloud layer. The moon takes just under twenty-seven hours to orbit Neptune.

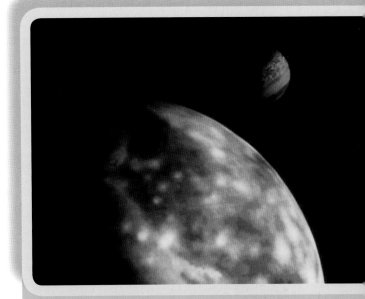

This image of Nereid was taken by *Voyager 2*. Neptune can be seen in the distance.

Nereid was discovered in 1949, long before *Voyager 2* discovered the other moons. It is Neptune's third-largest moon and was named after a Greek sea nymph. During its orbit, its distance from the planet can be anywhere from 841,100 to 5,980,200 miles (1,353,600 to 9,623,700 km). Because it is so far away from the planet, it takes about 360 days for Nereid to travel around Neptune.

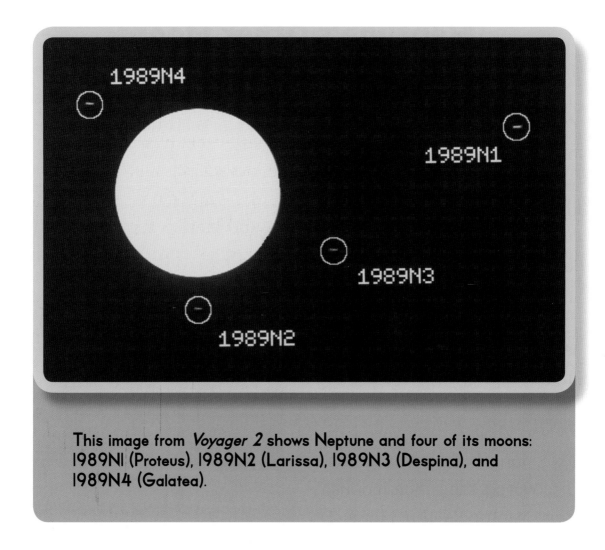

This image from *Voyager 2* shows Neptune and four of its moons: 1989N1 (Proteus), 1989N2 (Larissa), 1989N3 (Despina), and 1989N4 (Galatea).

In 1989, *Voyager 2* discovered five other Neptunian moons. From smallest to largest they are Larissa, Galatea, Despina, Thalassa, and Naiad. Like Triton and Nereid, the names of these moons comes from Greek mythology. Larissa, Galatea, and Despina were sea nymphs, and Naiad was a water spirit. Thalassa was the mother of the sea.

Halimede, Sao, Laomedeia, Psamathe and Neso

Since the *Voyager 2* observations, astronomers believed that Neptune had only eight moons. That was until 2004, when astronomer Matthew Holman and fellow scientists at the Center for Astrophysics found five new moons. Each moon was about 20 to 30 miles (32 to 48 km) across and circled the planet far outside the orbit of Nereid. All five moons were named after nereids (sea nymphs) in Greek mythology.

Halimede is 38 miles (61 km) across and is just under 10 billion miles (15 billion km) from Neptune. Sao, at 25 miles (40 km) across, is 14 billion miles (22 billion km) from Neptune. Laomedeia is the same size as Sao but is 14 billion miles (23 billion km) from Neptune. Psamathe is only 24 miles (38 km) across and is about 28 billion miles (46 billion km) from Neptune. Neso is

NEPTUNE'S ASTEROIDS?

There may be still more moons or at least bits of moons to be found. In 2001, NASA scientists located one asteroid, called a Trojan, in Neptune's shadow. Since 2006, astronomers have found at least four more Trojans. They suspect that there may be a whole cloud of them, possibly numbering in the hundreds, orbiting Neptune, but mostly hidden by the planet's shadow.

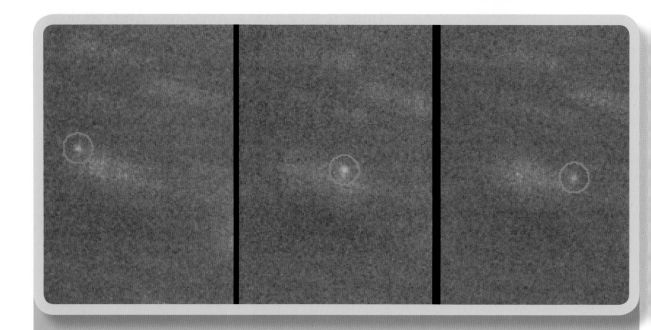

A ground-based telescope captured these images of three of Neptune's newest moons.

the outermost moon and is about 37 miles (60 km) across. It is 30 billion miles (49 billion km) from Neptune.

Like everything else about Neptune, these moons are unusual. Two of these odd little moons orbit in the normal forward direction, while three move backward, like giant Triton. However, it is hard to tell which moons are which because of the great distance and the moons' small size. The time it takes them to orbit Neptune ranges from five to twenty-five years. It has been suggested that these tiny moons are all that is left of a larger moon that was caught and torn apart by Triton's gravity. That may be why three go the "wrong way" around Neptune.

NEPTUNE'S RINGS

Voyager 2 showed images of Neptune's rings in 1989. There were four rings—one of them was faint and the other three were slightly easier to see. The faint one was named Galle after the German astronomer who had first seen Neptune through a telescope. The other three were named Le Verrier, Lassell, and Adams after the other discoverers of Neptune. Adams is the farthest ring, at 23,700 miles (62,930 km) from Neptune. Galle

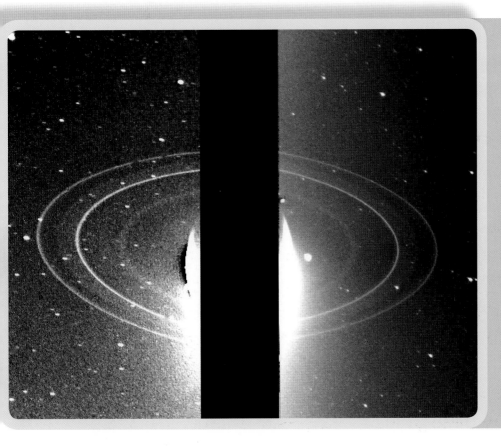

Two images from *Voyager 2* are put together to show how Neptune's rings encircle the planet.

THE W. M. KECK OBSERVATORY

The W. M. Keck Observatory, often called the Keck, stands at the top of Hawaii's dormant Mauna Kea volcano. At 13,796 feet (4,205 meters) high, it is a perfect place for a land-based telescope. Surrounded by miles of open ocean, there are no nearby mountain ranges or light pollution from cities to hinder the view. For most of the year, the atmosphere above Mauna Kea is clear, calm, and dry. There are actually two Keck Telescopes—twin instruments that are the world's largest optical and infrared telescopes. Keck I began operating in May 1993, and Keck II began operating in October 1996.

is the closest ring, at 10,600 miles (41,900 km) from Neptune. Unlike Saturn's rings, which are easy to see, Neptune's rings are difficult to see. They have bright sections, called arcs, and dark sections. Some of the rings even look braided, though that may be just a trick of the light and dark sections being seen together.

Since their 1989 discovery by *Voyager 2*, however, new images taken with the Keck telescope in Hawaii in 2002 and 2003 showed something unexpected. Some or possibly all of Neptune's rings may be slowly disappearing. Parts of them had already disappeared by 2002 and others seem to be fading. So far, astronomers have no theories about why the rings are disappearing. It may be that these rings are made of space dust that moves away or disintegrates. It may also be that—unlike other planets with rings, such as those around Uranus—Neptune may have no little **"shepherd moons"** in the rings to hold the rings together with their gravitational pull.

A close-up *Voyager 2* image of Neptune's rings, shows how parts are bright, while others appear faded. Current images from the Hubble Space Telescope show that Neptune's rings may be disappearing.

4

NEPTUNE'S PHYSICAL FEATURES

"Neptune is peculiar," says Craig Agnor, a scientist at the University of California, Santa Cruz. To many, that seems to be quite an understatement. Though it is a gas giant, like some other planets, Neptune is very different from the other seven planets in our Solar System.

Neptune is about 2.77 billion miles (4.46 billion km) from the Sun, which makes it very cold. Yet it has some mysterious source of energy, which powers winds that can blow up to 1,000 or 1,500 miles (1,600 to 2,000 km) per hour. This is faster than the winds on any other planet. Neptune is also a deeper, richer hue of blue

A striking image from *Voyager 2* shows Neptune's glowing rim. The blue-green color is from the methane in the planet's atmosphere.

than can be explained by methane in the atmosphere. The planet has rings that are mysteriously disappearing. And it has an icy moon—Triton—that still manages, despite its coldness, to have geysers.

THE HUBBLE SPACE TELESCOPE

Astronomers had known for some time that any Earth-based telescope was going to have a problem with interference from the Earth's atmosphere and with light pollution from cities.

In 1969, the United States Congress set aside money for a telescope that would stay in orbit around the Earth. This space-based telescope would not have the distortions caused by the atmosphere and light from the cities, allowing us to clearly see objects in space.

It took almost ten years to build such a telescope. The Hubble Space Telescope experienced several delays

The Hubble Space Telescope has provided scientists with some of the clearest images of outer space that have ever been seen.

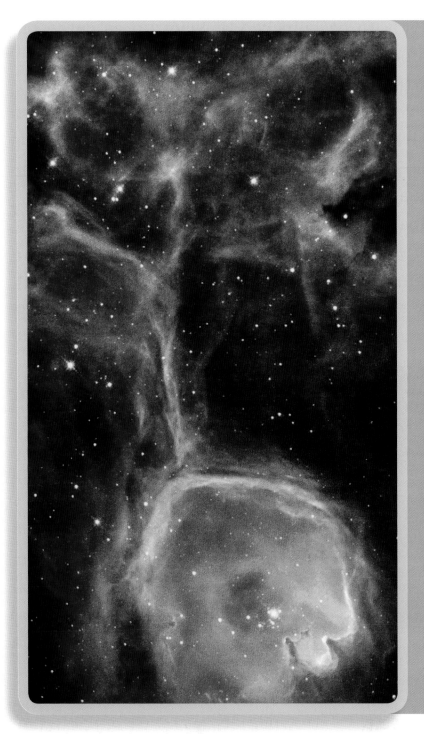

The Hubble is used to view planets, stars, moons, galaxies, and other space objects as they move through space. This image from the Hubble shows a rare view of a gas cavity that is being carved by stellar (star) winds and intense radiation from a hot star.

before it was ready to be launched. It went up as cargo on April 24, 1990, aboard the Space Shuttle *Discovery*. The shuttle astronauts placed it into its orbit in space on April 25.

When the Hubble needs to be fixed or maintained, astronauts must do the repairs. Because it has been kept in good condition, the Hubble Space Telescope has shown astronomers on Earth some amazing images of galaxies, stars, and planets.

The Hubble Space Telescope has also shown astronomers that Neptune is a very active planet. The weather on Neptune is constantly changing. Hubble images have shown that the Great Dark Spot is now gone, as though that storm had ended. There

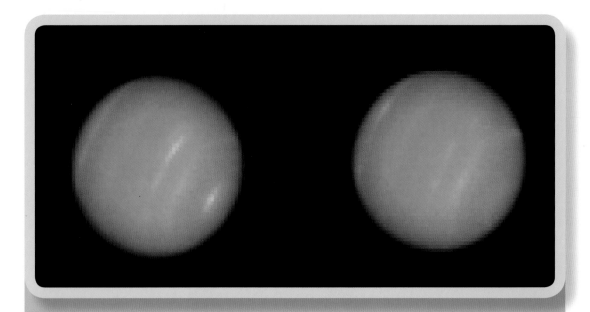

The Hubble Space Telescope took these two images of the planet in 1994. At the time, these were the clearest images of Neptune since *Voyager 2* flew by in 1989.

COMPARING NEPTUNE AND EARTH

	NEPTUNE	EARTH
DISTANCE FROM THE SUN	2.77 billion miles (4.46 billion km)	93 million miles (149.6 million km)
DIAMETER	30,760 miles (49,493 km)	7,926 miles (12,756 km)
AVERAGE TEMPERATURE	-346 degrees Fahrenheit (-210 degrees C)	60 degrees Fahrenheit (15 degrees C)
LENGTH OF YEAR	165 Earth years	365 days
LENGTH OF DAY	17.24 hours	24 hours
NUMBER OF MOONS	13	1
COMPOSITION OF PLANET	Hydrogen, methane, ammonia, and water	Mostly metals and rock
ATMOSPHERE	Methane and nitrogen	Mostly nitrogen and oxygen

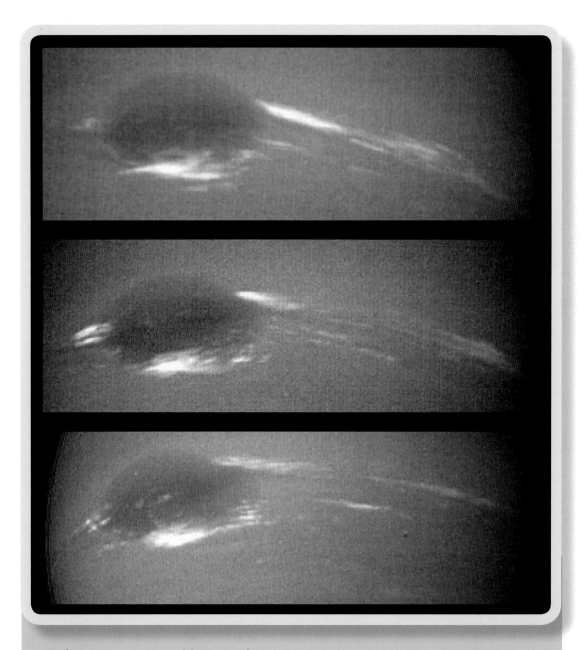

Images taken by *Voyager 2* helped scientists monitor changes in Neptune's weather, usually by tracking the clouds and apparent storms, like the Great Dark Spot shown here. Newer images from the Hubble Space Telescope have helped scientists further understand how the planet is changing.

The Hubble Space Telescope provided three views of Neptune's changing weather conditions. The pink areas shown here are clouds made of methane ice crystals. They move around the planet or disappear as the storms change.

was another, similar spot in Neptune's northern hemisphere in 1994, but that storm ended in 1997. The Hubble Space Telescope continues to send back images of Neptune's rapidly changing weather.

NEPTUNE'S INTERIOR

The eight planets in our Solar System can be divided into **terrestrial**, or rocky, planets or gas giants. Earth, Mercury, Venus, and Mars are all terrestrial planets. Jupiter, Saturn, Uranus, and Neptune are gas giants.

Our Solar System is made up of eight planets: the terrestrial planets, Mercury, Venus, Earth, and Mars, and the gas giants Jupiter, Saturn, Uranus, and Neptune. Pluto used to be considered the ninth planet, but in 2006 it was reclassified as a dwarf planet.

Neptune seems to be made up of hydrogen, methane, ammonia, and water. For almost a hundred years, scientists had assumed that rock accounted for most of Neptune's **core**. If this was true, it would mean that Neptune is more like Earth than the other gas giants. But when *Voyager 2* passed close to Neptune, its data strongly suggested that Neptune's core had a relatively low density—about that of water. This meant that the core probably was not made of rock or metals, since that would result in a higher density.

Scientists at the Lawrence Livermore National Laboratory in California tested this by creating what they called a planet in a bottle. This was a mix of water, ammonia, and alcohol, which imitated what they believed Neptune's core might be like. Through experiments, they discovered that the planet might indeed have a liquid core, either of water or liquefied gases—gases turned to liquid under pressure, such as hydrogen. This would make Neptune more like Uranus than Earth.

Scientists are not quite sure what Neptune's core is made of. Density readings, however, suggest that the core is not rocky as once supposed. Instead, it is most likely made up of liquefied elements like hydrogen. This illustration also shows how Earth compares in size to Neptune.

THE AMAZING SPACE TELESCOPE

The Hubble Space Telescope is meant to be used by just about anyone from around the world. An astronomer can submit a research proposal and ask for time on the telescope. Experts then determine which of the proposals to approve and allow those astronomers to use the telescope. Once the observations are made, an astronomer has up to a year in which to publish his or her findings. After one year, the observations are made public to all astronomers. So far, more than six thousand science articles have been published using data from the Hubble Space Telescope.

TEMPERATURE

The first temperature map of Neptune's lower atmosphere was created in early 2007 with the help of the European Southern Observatory's Very Large Telescope in Paranal, Chile. The map shows that Neptune's south pole is about 50 degrees Fahrenheit (10 degrees C) warmer than any other place on the planet. The average temperature of the atmosphere's lower depths is -392 degrees Fahrenheit (-200 degrees C). The planet's south pole is warm enough for methane gas to rise into the upper atmosphere.

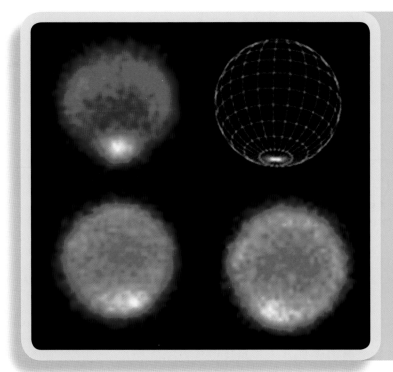

Thermal images taken in 2006 by the Very Large Telescope in Chile, show that Neptune's south pole is a lot warmer than the rest of the planet.

It may be that the difference in temperature between the warmer south pole and the rest of the planet is what causes Neptune's powerful winds. The Hubble has shown images of white clouds continuing to race across the planet's surface, which serves as proof of these strong winds.

Studies of Neptune show that the cloudy surface of the planet's southern hemisphere is brightening and absorbing more sunlight. The clouds have been brightening since 1980. This could be a sign that Neptune has different seasons, like most other planets do. Unlike Earth's seasons, however, Neptune's seasons would last decades instead of months.

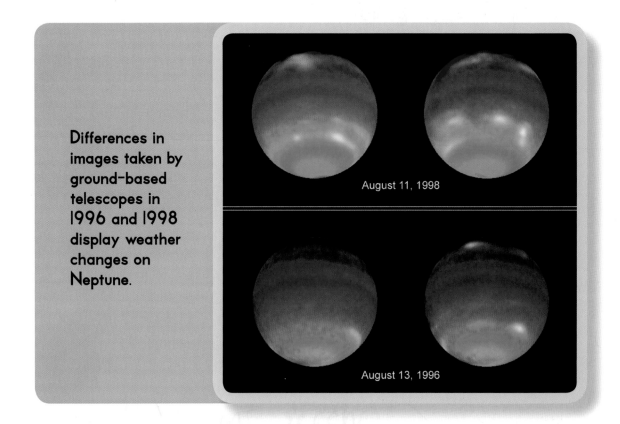

Differences in images taken by ground-based telescopes in 1996 and 1998 display weather changes on Neptune.

August 11, 1998

August 13, 1996

LIFE ON NEPTUNE

It is hard for scientists to know if life exists on Neptune. The planet's cold temperatures and methane and nitrogen atmosphere would make it hard for life-forms—the ones that we are familiar with, anyway—to survive. Some scientists think that life could exist below the surface of other planets. But Neptune's hot, liquefied interior makes that unlikely. Scientists are also not sure if water exists in the planet or in its atmosphere, though many theorize that there is none.

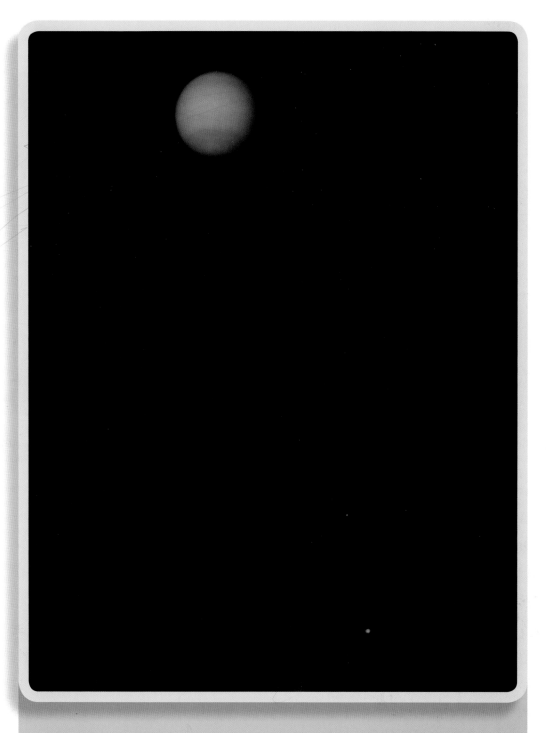

Voyager 2 provided scientists with a lot of data and many images of Neptune and its moons (Triton is shown here at the bottom right), but whether or not life exists on the planet is still a mystery.

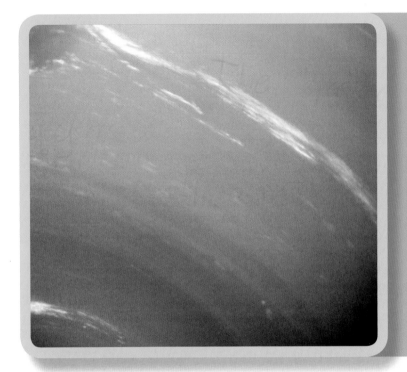

A close-up view of the swiftly moving Neptunian clouds shows that the planet's atmosphere may be too violent and stormy for life to exist.

MISSIONS TO NEPTUNE

It is hard for spacecraft to travel to Neptune since it is so far away, and scientists are not sure if a mission to Neptune will happen anytime soon. The Hubble Space Telescope continues to provide images of the planet, and spacecraft heading beyond our Solar System may also be able to observe Neptune. One example is the *New Horizons* spacecraft. In October 2007, the spacecraft, which is on its way to the dwarf planet Pluto, was able to obtain images of Triton and Neptune from 2.33 billion miles (3.75 billion km) away.

New space technology and new discoveries about Neptune may one day reveal more of Neptune's secrets.

Until new missions to Neptune occur, observations will have to be made through telescopes and calculations. Perhaps it will fall to some young astronomer, just as it did to John Couch Adams, to discover something new and amazing about the eight planet.

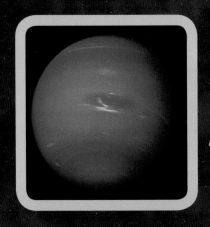

QUICK FACTS ABOUT NEPTUNE

DISCOVERY: 1845 to 1846 by John Couch Adams and Urbain J. J. Le Verrier

SOURCE OF NAME: Roman god of the sea

AVERAGE DISTANCE FROM THE SUN: 2.77 billion miles (4.46 billion km)

AVERAGE DISTANCE FROM EARTH: 2.68 billion miles (4.3 billion km)

TYPE OF PLANET: Gas giant

DIAMETER: 30,760 miles (49,493 km)

NEPTUNE DAY: 17.24 hours

NEPTUNE YEAR: 165 Earth years

AVERAGE TEMPERATURE: -346 degrees Fahrenheit (-210 degrees C)

MOONS: Thirteen: Naiad, Thalassa, Despina, Galatea, Larissa, Proteus, Triton, Nereid, Halimede, Sao, Laomedeia, Psamathe, Neso

RINGS: Four: Galle, Le Verrier, Lassall, Adams

GLOSSARY

asteroid—A rocky body that mainly orbits the Sun and is usually found between Mars and Jupiter.

astronomers—Scientists who study planets, stars, galaxies, and other objects in space.

atmosphere—A layer of gases that surrounds a planet.

aviation—The art or science of operating aircraft.

axis—An imaginary straight line going through the center of a planet or other celestial body. The planet or celestial body rotates around its axis.

Big Bang theory—A theory that the universe began with one great burst of energy.

core—The central part of a planet.

dwarf planet—A celestial body— but not a moon—that orbits the Sun with enough mass to be rounded by its own gravity, but cannot clear its region of smaller celestial bodies.

galaxy—A group of stars, dust, and gas held together by gravity. Our Solar System is in the Milky Way galaxy.

gas giant—One of the four outermost planets, mostly made up of gas.

geysers – On Earth, natural hot springs that send plumes of water and steam into the air. Neptune's geysers are made of nitrogen and methane.

gravity—A force that attracts one object to another. Objects with more mass have stronger gravitational pull on other objects. Distance between objects can also affect gravity.

Great Dark Spot—A giant storm on Neptune, which was first viewed by *Voyager 2,* but is now gone.

heliopause—The space outside the Sun's influence.

infrared telescope—A telescope that uses infrared rays (waves of light beyond the visible spectrum) to view distant objects.

Kuiper Belt—A disc-shaped zone about 2.8 to 4.6 billion miles (4.5 to 7.4 billion km) from the Sun. The belt has icy bodies that orbit the Sun outside Neptune's orbit.

light pollution—Light—usually artificial light from cities or other human-made structures—that interferes with viewing space objects in the night sky.

magnetic field—A field of force where magnetism affects other forces or objects in the field. Magnetic fields around planets determine the position of the planet's poles and may also block energy, wind, and particles from the Sun or from space.

NASA—The National Aeronautics and Space Administration is the official space agency of the United States.

optical telescope—A telescope that uses lenses or mirrors to form and magnify an image.

orbit—The set path that a planet, moon, or other celestial body takes around another object in space.

retrograde—Moving in a backward direction.

satellite— An object that orbits a larger body. Satellites can be natural, such as a moon, or human-made, such as the Hubble Space Telescope.

shepherd moons—Small moons found within a planet's rings. The gravitational forces of these moons may keep the ring material together.

terrestrial— Relating to land rather than to the sea or atmosphere.

FIND OUT MORE

BOOKS

Aguilar, David. *11 Planets: A New View of the Solar System*. Washington, D.C.: National Geographic Society, 2008.

Barnes-Svarney, Patricia. *A Traveler's Guide to the Solar System*. New York, NY: Sterling Publishing, 2008.

Bortz, Fred. *Beyond Jupiter: The Story of Planetary Astronomer Heidi Hammel*. New York: Franklin Watts, 2005.

Crosswell, Ken. *Ten Worlds: Everything that Orbits the Sun*. Honesdale, PA: Boyds Mills Press, 2007.

Elkins-Tanton, Linda. *Uranus, Neptune, Pluto, and the Outer Solar System*. New York: Facts on File, 2006.

Jenkins, Alvin. *Next Stop, Neptune: Experiencing the Solar System*. Boston: Houghton Mifflin, 2004.

Mist, Rosalind. *Uranus, Neptune, and the Dwarf Planets*. Mankato, MN: QEB Publishing, 2009.

Scherer, Glenn, and Marty Fletcher. *Neptune*. Berkeley Heights, NJ: MyReportLinks.com Books, 2005.

Slade, Suzanne. *A Look at Neptune*. New York: PowerKids Press, 2008.

World Book, *Neptune and the Distant Dwarf Planets*. Chicago: World Book, 2007.

WEBSITES

CoolCosmos: Neptune
http://coolcosmos.ipac.caltech.edu/cosmic_kids/AskKids/neptune.shtml

Curious about Astronomy? Ask an Astronomer
http://curious.astro.cornell.edu

ESA-KIDS: Neptune
http://www.esa.int/esaKIDSen/SEM7CTMZCIE_OurUniverse_o.html

HubbleSite
http://hubblesite.org

NASA Kids' Club
http://www.nasa.gov/audience/forkids/kidsclub/flash/index.html

NASA: Neptune
http://www.nasa.gov/worldbook/neptune_worldbook.html

NASA Solar System Exploration for Kids
http://solarsystem.nasa.gov/kids/index.cfm

The ~~Nine~~ 8 Planets—Just for Kids
http://kids.nineplanets.org

Science News for Kids: Strange Neptune
http://www.sciencenewsforkids.org/articles/20070117/Feature1.asp

Voyager: The Interstellar Mission
http://voyager.jpl.nasa.gov

Welcome to the Planets: Neptune
http://pds.jpl.nasa.gov/planets/choices/neptune1.htm

BIBLIOGRAPHY

The author found these resources especially helpful while researching this book.

Beatty, J. Kelly et al. *The New Solar System.* New York: Cambridge University Press, 1999.

Clark, Stuart. "How Neptune Snagged a Passing Moon." *New Scientist* 2551 (2006): 8.

Corfield, Richard. *Lives of the Planets: A Natural History of the Solar System.* New York: Basic Books, 2007.

Cowen, Ron. "Neptune's Balmy South Pole." http://www.sciencenews.org/view/generic/id/8980/title/Neptunes_balmy_south_pole

Eberhart, Jonathan. "Triton's Geysers: Solar-powered Scenario." http://www.thefreelibrary.com/Triton's+geysers%3a+solar-powered+scenario-a08879005

Miller, Ron and William K. Hartmann. *The Grand Tour: A Traveler's Guide to the Solar System.* New York: Workman Publishing, 2005.

Science News. "Neptune: A Watery Planet at Heart." http://www.articlearchives.com/trends-events/investigations/258661-1.html

New Scientist. "Neptune's Hidden Asteroid Belt." http://www.newscientist.com/article/mg19025575.800-neptunes-hidden-asteroid-belt.html

---. "Neptune's Rings Are Fading Away." http://www.newscientist.com/article/mg18524925.900-neptunes-rings-are-fading-away.html

Price, Fred W. *The Planet Observer's Handbook.* New York: Cambridge University Press, 2000.

Sobel, Dana. *The Planets.* New York: Viking, 2005.

Thomas, Vanessa. "Neptune's Signs of Spring." *Astronomy* 9: 32.

Windows to the Universe. "Three New Moons Found Around Neptune." http://www.windows.ucar.edu/tour/link=/headline_universe/neptune_newmoons.html&text=t

INDEX

ABOUT THE AUTHOR

Josepha Sherman has written everything from fantasy novels to science books and short articles about quantum mechanics for elementary school students.